This Disney Princess
Annual belongs to

....

Annual 2011

EGMONT
We bring stories to life

First published in Great Britain 2010
by Egmont UK Limited,
239 Kensington High Street, London W8 6SA

Group Art Editor: Jeanette Ryall • Group Editor: Keilly Swift
• Art Editor: Amanda Hartley • Designers: Clare Marshall, Anni Nolan • Writer: Olivia McLearon

© 2010 Disney Enterprises, Inc.

ISBN 978 1 4052 5249 2
1 3 5 7 9 10 8 6 4 2
Printed in Italy

All of this inside...

Welcome to ... Tiana's World

Fun and fiesty, Tiana is also super-talented ... whether she's a human or a frog!

Story Time

Tiana and her best friend Charlotte have known each other since they were little. They loved *The Frog Prince* story, but Tiana said she'd NEVER, ever kiss a frog!

Big Dream

Tiana's daddy was a great cook and he taught Tiana everything he knew. He inspired Tiana's big dream to open her very own restaurant.

Top Tiana Moments

Tiana being taken by surprise when she meets Prince Naveen, the talking frog!

Tiana being persuaded to kiss Prince Naveen . . . and turning into a frog herself!

Tiana, as a frog, realising that she has fallen in love with Prince Naveen.

"Just one kiss."

Your Talent

Tiana has a talent for cooking.
What are you good at doing?

....

Tiana dreams of opening her own restaurant.
What do you want to do when you grow up?

....

Tiana & Friends

Meet the characters who are part of Tiana's incredible journey. Tick the boxes to show if each one is a friend or a foe!

Louis

is a trumpet-playing alligator who loves jazz. He dreams of becoming a human, and makes friends with Tiana and Naveen during their amazing adventure.

Friend   Foe

Dr Facilier

is a mysterious, menacing man, who uses magical spells to his advantage. He uses evil shadows to help him with his mean plans, which involve Tiana and Naveen!

Friend   Foe

Charlotte

is Tiana's best friend. She grew up dreaming of marrying a prince. She can be spoilt and demanding, but would do anything for her best friend, Tiana.

Friend   Foe

Ray

Charming, gentle and romantic, Ray is a sweet firefly who helps Tiana and Naveen. He's also totally in love with Evangeline, who he thinks is a firefly, but is actually a star.

Friend   Foe

Lawrence

works for Prince Naveen. He's secretly jealous of his master, because he's carefree and handsome. So Lawrence joins forces with a powerful man, with shocking results!

Friend   Foe

Mama Odie

Wild and witty, Mama Odie, is 197 years old! She lives with her pet snake, Juju, and uses magic. Unlike Dr Facilier, she uses her magic to help those in need.

Friend   Foe

Naveen

is a charming, handsome prince from Maldonia. He loves jazz music, so moves to New Orleans, the home of jazz. But Naveen doesn't count on getting tricked by the shady Dr Facilier.

Friend   Foe

Kiss the Frog

Shout out the picture words as you read the story, using the key below.

 was at a costume party, standing out on the

balcony and feeling sad. She looked down and

suddenly saw a sitting on the edge of the

balcony. "I reckon you want a kiss!" said

chuckling. "Kissing would be … nice," grinned

Character Key

Naveen   Tiana   Frog

12

the 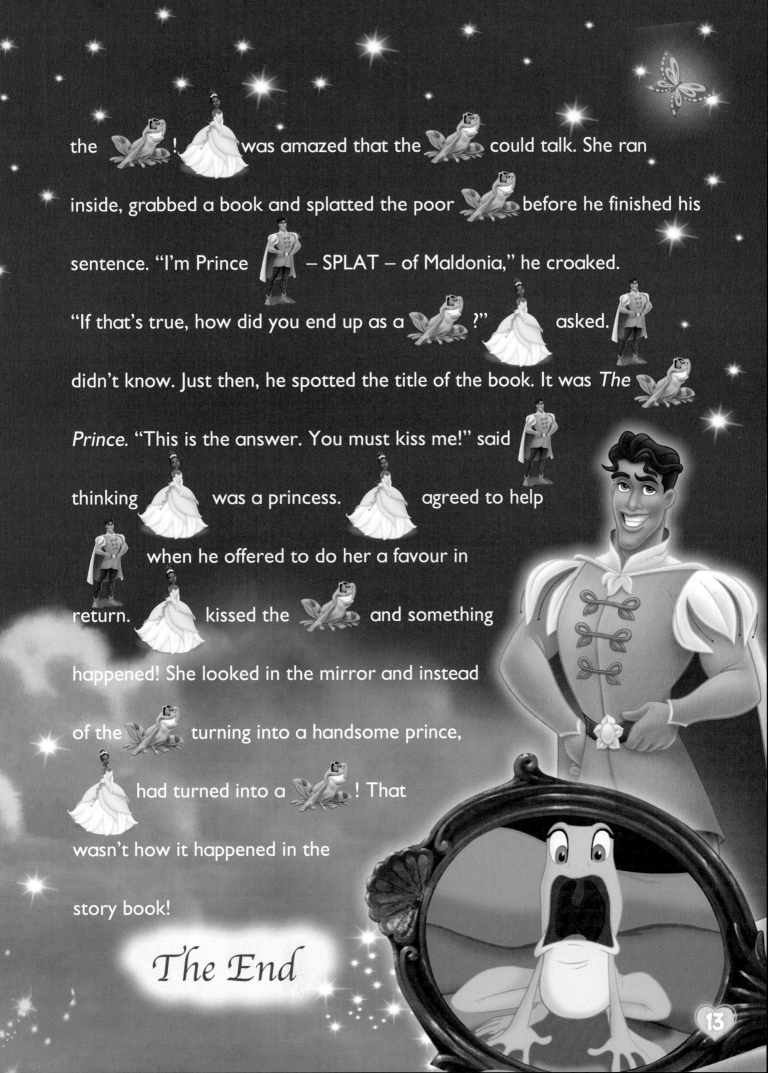! 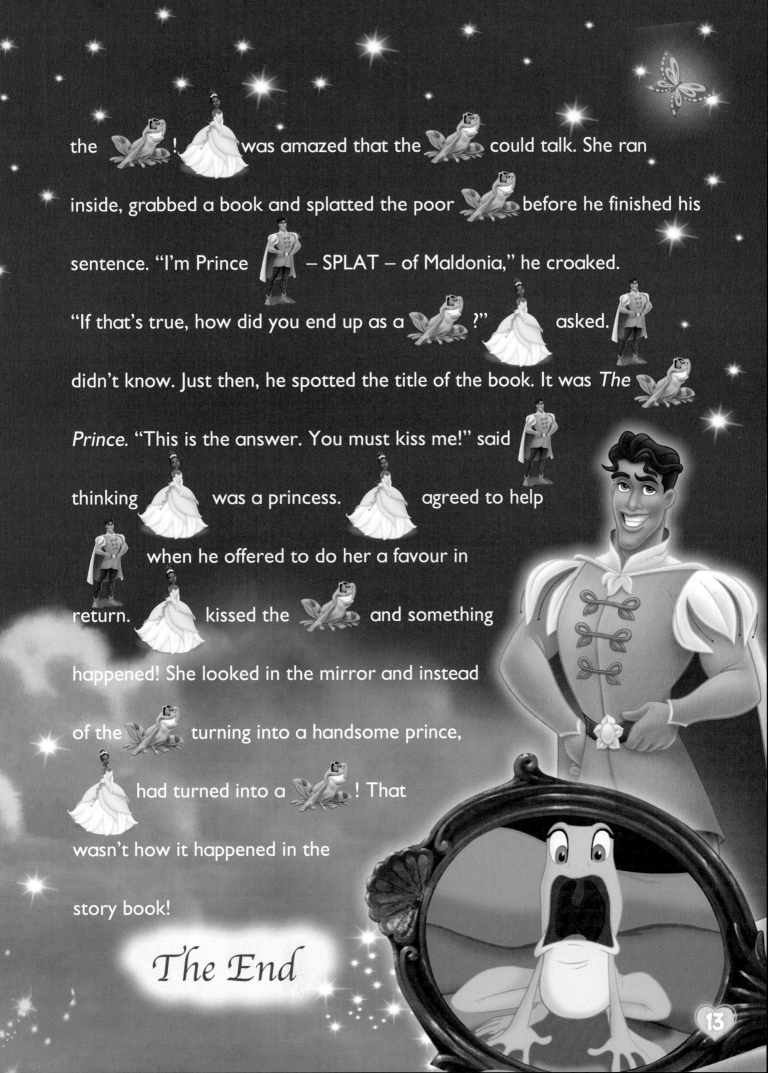 was amazed that the could talk. She ran

inside, grabbed a book and splatted the poor before he finished his

sentence. "I'm Prince – SPLAT – of Maldonia," he croaked.

"If that's true, how did you end up as a ?" asked.

didn't know. Just then, he spotted the title of the book. It was *The*

Prince. "This is the answer. You must kiss me!" said

thinking was a princess. agreed to help

 when he offered to do her a favour in

return. kissed the and something

happened! She looked in the mirror and instead

of the turning into a handsome prince,

 had turned into a ! That

wasn't how it happened in the

story book!

The End

Fun with Tiana

Can you help Tiana solve these puzzles?

Shadow Princess
Which of these shadows matches Tiana?

a

b

c

d

Spot the Difference
Can you spot which picture of Ray is the odd one out?

a

b

c

Funny Frog

Doctor Facilier has turned Prince Naveen into a frog! Unscramble the words to work out what Naveen is saying.

I ~v~ole ~z~jaz

_ _ _ U _ _ _ Z _

Who's Who?

Draw a line to match each name to the picture of the right character.

✳ Tiana

✳ Naveen

✳ Charlotte

✳ Mama Odie

a

b

c

d

Floating Lily

Create your own pretty lily decorations.

You will need
* Scissors
* Green felt tip pen
* Pink shredded paper
* Polystyrene cup

1

To make your lily, ask an adult to help you cut the cup into a lily shape, just like this.

2

Colour the inside base of the lily with a green marker. Fill the lily with shredded pink paper. Place the lily in a bowl of water and watch it float!

Perfect Princess

Colour in this beautiful picture of Tiana with your favourite pens.

Welcome to ...
Belle's World

Find out all about beautiful Belle, the peasant girl who stole the heart of the Beast.

All about Belle

Hair colour: Brown
Eye colour: Brown
Favourite outfit: Yellow ballroom dress
Hobbies: Reading and Dancing

"Belle is thoughtful, romantic and very kind-hearted."

" He was mean and unrefined, but now he's dear and unsure."

The Beast

When Belle first met the Beast, she thought he was mean and grumpy, but she soon saw a different side to him and they fell in love.

Belle broke the spell on the Beast by falling in love with him before the enchanted rose lost its petals.

Magical Wardrobe

Belle is lucky enough to have the Wardrobe to help her decide what dresses to wear every day. Find out her favourite outfit in her fact file.

All about you

Fill in the details about yourself:

Hair colour: Blondy-brown

Eye colour: brown

Favourite outfit:

Hobbies: Writing, reading, Art

Amazing Friends

Lumiere, Cogsworth, Mrs Potts and Chip are the Beast's loyal servants and friends. Belle will never forget how they helped her to see his softer side!

19

Beautiful Belle

Belle looks gorgeous in her ballgown. Can you spot the five differences between these two pictures?

Colour in a heart as you spot each one.

Dress Dash

Which path should Belle take to get to the Wardrobe and all her lovely dresses?

Start

a

b

c

21

The Perfect Match

Belle and the Beast are planning a party,
but not everything goes to plan ...

1 It was Belle and the Beast's first anniversary and they both had the perfect idea for how to celebrate.

2 Unfortunately, their ideas were totally different! The Beast really didn't want a pink themed party!

3 "Why don't we combine our ideas to make the perfect party?" suggested Belle. "Could you help us?" she asked Mrs Potts, Lumiere, Cogsworth and Chip.

4 Mrs Potts started helping Belle with her party food. "This is going to be hard," she muttered, "they want totally different things!"

5 "It's going to end in tears," thought Mrs Potts, as she finished off the Beast's delicious chocolate cake.

6 Meanwhile, Chip was helping Belle rehearse her special party song. "It's wonderful," he chirped.

7 Next, it was the Beast's turn. He practised his piano piece, but as soon as he started to sing, it sounded awful! Was this party a good idea?

9 "I've composed a tune for you, Belle," the Beast said as he sat down at the piano. "It's to thank you for the most wonderful year of my life." Chip was worried!

9 The Beast started playing. His music suited Belle's voice and lyrics perfectly! Chip was so excited, he started jumping up and down on the piano!

10 Belle and the Beast smiled as they looked around them. "Happy anniversary," smiled Belle. "Our ideas worked so well, I think we really are the perfect match," the Beast grinned!

The End

Colour Me Beautiful

Join the dots to complete the picture of Belle
and her friends, then colour it in!

Welcome to ... Aurora's World

Find out all about lovely Aurora and share your dreams with her.

Peasant Girl

Aurora was raised in the woods as a peasant girl named Briar Rose. She was lonely at times, but the forest animals became her great friends.

Waking Up

After pricking her finger on a spinning wheel, Aurora fell into a very deep sleep. She was woken by Prince Phillip's kiss and they have loved each other ever since!

"If you dream a thing more than once, it's sure to come true!"

Fairy Friends

Flora, Fauna and Merryweather are Aurora's fairy godmothers and they always look out for her. When Aurora was born, they each gave her a special gift.

Trace your finger along the fairies' trail and make a wish!

Beautiful Dream

Aurora must have had amazing dreams when she was sleeping! Have you had any beautiful dreams? Use this space to write about your favourite dream ever.

....

....

....

....

Sing-a-long with Aurora

Aurora loves to sing! Join Aurora in this magical song for her animal friends.

Aurora's Song

Singing fills my heart with joy,
It really makes me glad,
I love singing to animals,
Especially when they're sad.

Singing songs is so much fun,
so much fun, so much fun!
(Repeat once)

Singing makes my friends smile too,
They love to whistle along,
Singing is the most beautiful thing,
So join me when I sing this song.

Singing songs is so much fun,
so much fun, so much fun!
(Repeat once)

Sing loudly and clearly. You can use a microphone if you want to.

Use your finger to follow the musical trail, then colour in the musical notes!

2

Can you spot Flora, Fauna and Merryweather on the page? Tick the heart when you've found them.

1

How many squirrels are listening to Aurora sing? Write the answer in the heart.

Answers: 1. Three squirrels. 2. Flora is behind the tree on the right. Fauna is in front of Aurora in the middle of the page and Merryweather is in the top left corner.

The Cake Competition

Shout out the picture words as you read
the story, using the key below.

 loved baking cakes, so she was very excited when a Royal cake baking competition was announced. "What cake will you make?" asked her.

"You could bake a heart-shaped cake," interupted. "Or a diamond-shaped cake!" suggested .

"I'll think about what to make. I'm going to meet Prince Phillip now. Goodbye!" replied excitedly. Her fairy godmothers decided to work their magic and make a cake instead. But started waving her wand around in excitement and the

Key

Aurora

Flora

Fauna

Merryweather

30

multi-coloured icing went flying everywhere. Suddenly,  walked back into the room and, at that very moment, a dollop of icing landed on her brand new tiara!

"We're so sorry!"  gasped.

"Actually, you've just given me the perfect idea,"  giggled. It was a few days later and the cake competition day had arrived.  wowed the judges with her tiara cake. She was awarded first prize!

"Thank you so much," she smiled.

"I couldn't have done it without my fantastic fairy friends though!"

The End

Aurora's Puzzles

Can you complete Aurora's magical princess puzzles?

The Missing Pieces

Part of this Aurora picture is missing! Can you work out which pieces below are the missing parts?

1

2

a b c d

Add some pretty colours to Flora, Fauna and Merryweather!

Royal Dance

There are five differences in the second picture of Aurora and her Prince. Colour a flower as you find each one.

a

b

M
N I A
A
L S

Favourite Thing

Unscramble the letters to reveal something that Aurora loves.

A _ _ _ _ _ _

Welcome to ...
Jasmine's World

Find out all about Jasmine, the brainy and beautiful princess of Agrabah.

The Adventure Starts

Jasmine could never have imagined the adventures she was about to have when she bumped into Aladdin and Abu in the market. Now they're her best friends in the world!

Genius Genie

If it wasn't for the Genie, Aladdin and Jasmine probably would never have seen each other again. He's a true friend and he's really funny, too!

"It's all so magical."

Flying free

Aladdin and Jasmine fell in love when they went on a magical carpet ride together around the world. Jasmine loves to have adventures and to feel free!

Magic Carpet Ride

Imagine you're about to set off on a magical carpet ride!

Where would you go? ....

....

Who would you go with? ....

Draw a picture here ...

Jasmine's pet tiger, Rajah, is her best friend in the palace. He is very protective of her!

35

Jasmine's Garden

The colour has disappeared from some of Jasmine's flowers. Play this game to put the colour back into her garden and help her find her friends, too.

Can you find Jasmine's friend, Rajah, hidden on this page? Tick the box.

How many butterflies can you see on this page? Fill in the answer.

Player 1

Number of flowers coloured in

Answers: Rajah is tucked behind the big orange flower pot and there are two butterflies on the page.

How to play

You will need: A coin, colouring pens/pencils and a friend to play with. Take one page each, then take it in turns to close your eyes and drop a coin onto your page. If the coin lands on a flower, colour it in. If it lands on a question, answer it. Whoever completes all of their tasks first, wins!

How many butterflies can you see on this page? Fill in the answer.

Can you find Aladdin's monkey friend, Abu, hidden on this page? Tick the box.

Player 2

Number of flowers coloured in

37

The Magic Mirror

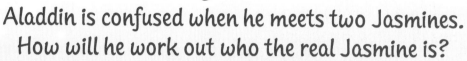

Aladdin is confused when he meets two Jasmines. How will he work out who the real Jasmine is?

Aladdin spotted his beautiful princess Jasmine in the courtyard. She was wearing his favourite purple outfit. He wanted to surprise her with some flowers he'd picked especially for her. However, Jasmine had her own surprise for Aladdin.

A second Jasmine suddenly appeared from behind a pillar! She was just as beautiful as the first Jasmine, but she wore an outfit made from blue silk. Aladdin felt confused. "One of us is the real Jasmine and the other is just a reflection which came out of a magic mirror!" the Jasmines explained to him.

"Then how do I know which one of you to give flowers to?" Aladdin asked. "You'll have to work out which of us is the real Jasmine," they replied together.

Aladdin wondered what he could do. "I know! Jasmine can sing beautifully. Please sing for me," he asked them. Both Jasmines started to sing for Aladdin, and each sang as brilliantly as the other.

Aladdin had to think of something else. "Jasmine is a wonderful dancer. Please dance for me!" he laughed. Again, both Jasmines danced incredibly well, so Aladdin could not tell them apart! "I really don't know which of you is the real Jasmine, so I will have to give my flowers to both of you," he said.

Aladdin divided his bunch of flowers in half. The Jasmine in purple stepped forward. "Please give the flowers to the other Jasmine. I would be happy for her to have them," she said kindly. "You've answered my question," Aladdin cried, as he wrapped his arms around the princess in purple. "You are the real Jasmine." "How did you know it was me?" she gasped. "You may both look the same, but it's what's inside that counts," Aladdin replied, smiling a huge smile!

The End

Jasmine & Friends

Tick your five favourite pictures to find out which of Jasmine's friends you are most like.

Mostly purple
You're brave, adventurous and kind. You dream of visiting new places and discovering new things, just like Aladdin.

Mostly pink
You're faithful, loyal and a good listener. Like Rajah, you love spending time with your best friend.

Mostly green
You're full of life and love having fun. Like Abu, you enjoy playing games with your friends.

A Perfect Pair

Use the colour key to help you brighten up this picture of Jasmine and Aladdin.

Key

Welcome to ... Ariel's World

Find out all about Ariel and explore Atlantica, the enchanted kingdom where she lives.

Underwater Friends

Flounder, the fish, is Ariel's best friend. He loves going on adventures with her, which is annoying for poor crab, Sebastian, whose job is to look after Ariel.

True Love

On one of Ariel's adventures, she visited the ocean surface. This was where she first saw Prince Eric and fell head over fin in love with him!

Can you spot Sebastian, the crab? He's never too far away from Ariel!

"If I become human, I'll never be with my father or sisters again,"

Family Fun

Ariel lives with her father, King Triton, and her six elder sisters, Arista, Alana, Aquata, Andrina, Adella and Attina – all beginning with A!

My Family

Ariel would like to know about your family. Draw or stick a picture of them here.

Ariel's Door Hanger

Make this enchanting Ariel shell door hanger to hang on your bedroom door.

You will need:
- Pink and white card
- Scissors
- Glue
- Sequins
- Gems
- Ribbon

1 Cut out a shell shape from the pink card. Then stick a circle of white card in the middle of the shell.

2 Decorate with sequins and gems, then stick a small loop of ribbon to the back of the top of the shell. Write your name in the white circle!

Can you find the friendly seahorse?

Princess Ariel's Room

A Birthday Surprise

Can Ariel find the perfect present
for her father's birthday?

1 It was the day of King Triton's birthday and Ariel had been so busy, she had almost forgotten to get him a present! So she swam to a nearby antique stall to look for something special. "I need a birthday present for my father," Ariel told the antique seller.

2 "Why don't you make him a special birthday present?" the antique seller suggested, "with some magic sea dust?"

3 "All you have to do is blow the dust and wish," the seller said, handing Ariel a box filled with the magic sea dust. "But be sure to choose your wishes well, the dust won't last long."

4 Later, at King Triton's birthday party, Ariel's sisters were worried because everyone looked bored.

5 "I think I can help!" said Ariel, and she blew a puff of the special magic dust.

6 Suddenly, a wonderful big wheel appeared, with glittering seashell seats. "Fantastic!" cried Ariel's sisters.

7 Ariel then decided to blow a puff of magic sea dust over the bandstand.

8 The musicians suddenly appeared and began to play the most wonderful music.

9 Ariel looked into the box. "Oh no!" she thought. "I've used up all my magic sea dust and I haven't wished for a present for daddy!"

10 But when King Triton saw Ariel's box he was amazed! "You've found my first ever money box!" he cried. "I was wishing only the other day that I had kept it!"

11 "Thank you, Ariel. You couldn't have given me a better present for all the money in the world," King Triton said, hugging his daughter.

The End

Under the Sea

Ariel is collecting sea jewels with her friends. Tick off each character when you spot them in the picture.

Colour in the treasure chest to make it sparkle!

Shell Star

Add some gorgeous colours to this pretty picture of Ariel.

Welcome to ...
Cinderella's World

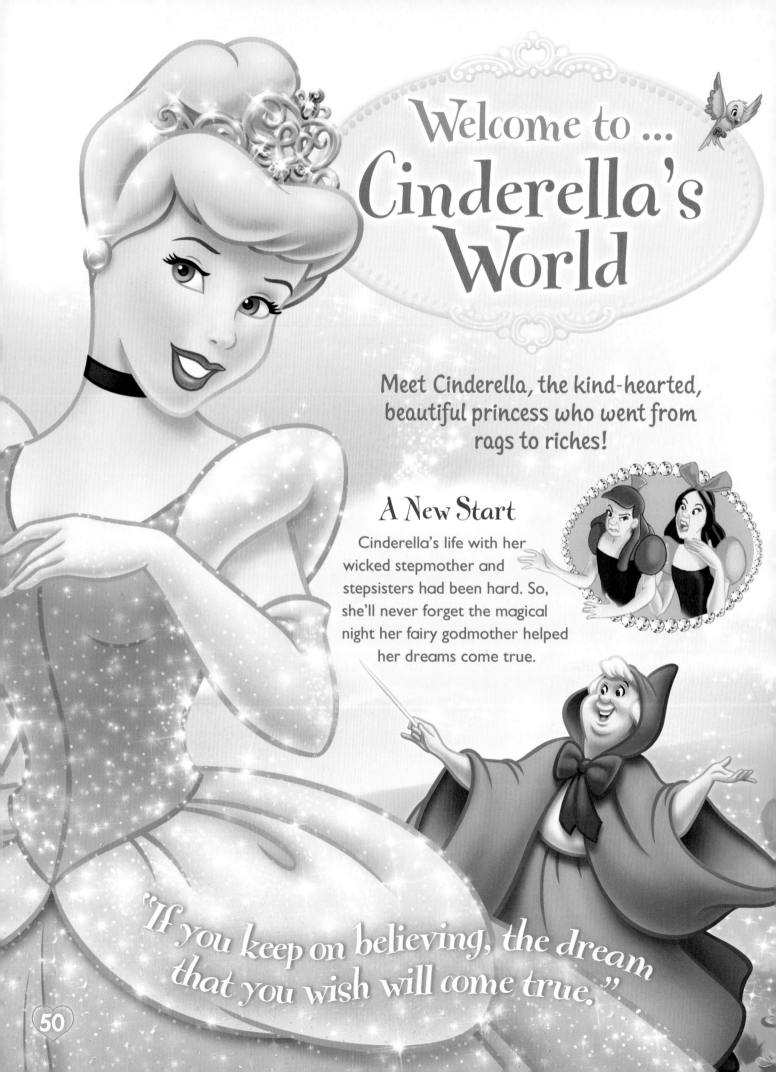

Meet Cinderella, the kind-hearted, beautiful princess who went from rags to riches!

A New Start

Cinderella's life with her wicked stepmother and stepsisters had been hard. So, she'll never forget the magical night her fairy godmother helped her dreams come true.

"If you keep on believing, the dream that you wish will come true."

Furry Friends

Cute mice, Gus and Jaq, are Cinderella's best friends. They have always been there to brighten her day and make her giggle!

Magical Ball

If you were having your own royal ball, who would you invite? Here's an idea for gorgeous invitations you could make for your friends.

True Love

Cinderella loves her life at the Royal Palace. She often thinks back to the night she met Prince Charming at the Royal Ball and to their beautiful wedding day at the palace.

Princess

To: ....

I'd love it if you could come to my magical Cinderella ball at:

....

Date: ....

Time: ....

Fancy dress code: Magical princess

Please RSVP

Love from: ....

You could photocopy the invitation to cut out and give to your friends.

Princess Playtime

Make your own wand and tiara, and you could
be just like Cinderella or her fairy godmother!

You will need:
Two pieces of blue ribbon,
safety scissors, a plain
headband and safe glue.

Cinderella Headband

1 Wrap a piece of
blue ribbon around
your headband. Use
scissors to trim it, then
glue into place.

2 Tie the other piece
of ribbon into a
pretty bow.

3 Stick the bow onto
the headband with glue.
When it's dry, you'll
have a perfect
Cinderella accessory!

Fairy Godmother Wand

You will need:
A pencil, silver foil, thick plain card, safety scissors and safe glue.

1 Wrap the silver foil tightly around the pencil.

2 Cut out two stars from the card, then cut out two star shapes from the silver foil. Stick the silver foil stars onto the card.

3 Use glue to carefully sandwich the end of the silver stick between the two silver stars.

The glass slipper has disappeared from this cushion. Can you find it on these pages?

53

A True Beauty

Cinderella is so excited about the palace beauty contest.
But will her stepsisters and stepmother ruin it?

Cinderella decided to make three special ballgowns for the beauty contest. She strolled through the palace grounds and felt inspired by everything she saw. The stunning colours of the peacock's tails and the roses in the garden gave her some wonderful ideas for her dresses. She walked through the kitchen and thought that the delicious cakes the chef was baking could be used as an idea for a dress, too!

"Remember, you have many other beautiful gowns if you don't manage to make these three," her fairy godmother said, appearing in front of her. Cinderella knew this was true, but she loved the idea of having three new gowns. So, she sketched her ideas and started making the gowns that afternoon. She had no idea that her stepsisters and stepmother had been secretly watching her.

The day of the beauty contest arrived and Cinderella was thinking about which one of her dresses to wear. Just then, her stepsisters and stepmother arrived, already dressed for the beauty contest.

"My stepmother's dress is very similar to mine ... oh," she gasped. "But, I don't

understand …" Lady Tremaine was wearing the green dress embroidered with real roses, which Cinderella had made the previous day. Next, Drizella strode across the stage in a beautiful bright blue dress, covered with real peacock feathers. It was the second dress Cinderella had spent hours creating. Finally, Anastacia appeared, wearing a pretty dress, covered in pink icing. It was the final dress that Cinderella had created for the contest.

"What shall I do?" she cried.

The Fairy Godmother suddenly appeared beside her. "It doesn't matter what you wear, it's inner beauty that counts," She said as she handed Cinderella her favourite white ballgown.

Cinderella walked down the carpet, trying to ignore her stepsisters' and stepmother's cruel comments, but their glee was short-lived. A group of birds descended on her stepmother, attracted by the roses on the dress. Bees swarmed around Anastacia's dress, drawn like a magnet to the sugar icing. Then the palace peacocks gathered around Drizella's dress and started plucking the feathers. As they shrieked in the background, the Prince appeared beside Cinderella with a crown.

"Cinderella, your true beauty always shines through," he said lovingly, as he fitted the crown on her head.

"My fairy godmother was right," Cinderella smiled to herself.

The End

Perfect Ponies

Tick the five pictures you like the most, then find out which pony would be your best friend!

Add some bright colours to the rosettes on this page.

Mostly Green

You love the countryside and fresh air. A pony who adores trekking, like this cutie, would be your perfect friend!

Mostly Blue

You're a loyal friend with tons of talent and enjoy spending time with your pals. This proud pony would be your best buddy.

Mostly Pink

Sparkling with confidence, you simply love to perform for your friends and family. This circus pony is truly the horse for you!

Sparkling Cinderella

Colour in this magical picture with your prettiest pens to make Cinderella really shine!

Welcome to ... Snow White's World

Take a peek inside Snow White's magical world and meet her many friends!

The magic mirror told the wicked Queen that Snow White was the fairest of all.

Woodland Animals

The forest animals love Snow White very much, especially when she sings to them. They led her through the forest when she was lost and have been her friends ever since.

"Anyone could see that the Prince was charming, the only one for me."

Tell Snow White all about your good friends.
Write their names here and add a picture!

My friends' names: ....

Stick a
picture here.

....

The Seven Dwarfs

When Snow White found a
cottage in the woods, she also
found seven great friends, the
Dwarfs Doc, Grumpy, Sleepy,
Bashful, Sneezy, Dopey
and Happy.

The Prince

Snow White was saved
by the Prince's kiss after
she had taken a bite of a
poisoned apple. Since that
day, she has lived happily
with her one true love.

Do you know
which Dwarf
is which?

Snow White Fun

Can you solve these sweet Snow White puzzles?

Which Path?

Help Snow White to find her way to Dopey and Sleepy and avoid all the poisonous apples along the way.

Start

Finish

A little bird needs some colour. Find him on these pages, then colour him in!

Find the Friends

Can you find the Seven Dwarfs' names in this grid? Colour an apple when you find each one.

Sneezy   Bashful

Sleepy   Grumpy

Doc   Dopey

Happy

X	P	K	Z	S	N	E	E	Z	Y
B	T	J	A	J	H	V	W	G	E
A	S	D	O	P	E	Y	K	H	C
S	K	G	R	U	M	P	Y	W	S
H	B	F	G	M	I	R	Z	T	L
F	T	G	O	E	B	Y	P	L	E
U	D	J	T	Y	R	S	D	H	E
L	O	D	E	S	I	S	Y	C	P
T	C	Q	H	A	P	P	Y	R	A
S	Y	I	B	X	T	Z	A	S	A

Forest Fun

There are five objects that don't belong in this pretty forest scene. Can you spot them?

Start

Finish

Helping Hands

Snow White and the Seven Dwarfs help her animal friends in their hour of need.

Snow White loved spending time in the beautiful palace gardens. They were completely captivating and near to the Dwarfs' cottage, as well as being near to the woods where her animal friends lived. Her woodland friends came to visit her every day at the same time without fail. They loved the gardens as much as she did.

One afternoon, Snow White walked towards the fountain where she always met the woodland animals and found that none of them were there! "How strange! Where could they be?" she wondered to herself. She wanted to find them in the forest, but had to get back to the palace for afternoon tea. "Never mind," she thought, "I'm sure they'll

be back tomorrow." But they weren't there the next day either. Snow White was confused, but then she realised the problem. "There's no water in the fountain. That's why the animals haven't visited me!" she told the Prince. Snow White felt so sad. What if it didn't rain for a long time?

Suddenly, she had a wonderful idea. "The Seven Dwarfs are sure to help me!" She rode to the Dwarfs' cottage and told them about the empty fountain and the

animals not being able to visit. Then she told them her brilliant idea. "We'd love to help!" they chorused.

Grumpy and Sneezy brought the ladder, while Bashful, Dopey, Sleepy and Happy brought along extra buckets. Doc went to fetch the animals. "I'll tell them we've got a big surprise for them!" he said excitedly. The Dwarfs set to work. By the time Doc arrived with the

animals, the fountain was running again! "What a brilliant idea this was, Snow White," the Prince said as he held her hand. "I couldn't have done it without the Seven Dwarfs though," she smiled, as the animals and birds gathered by the fountain happily!

The End

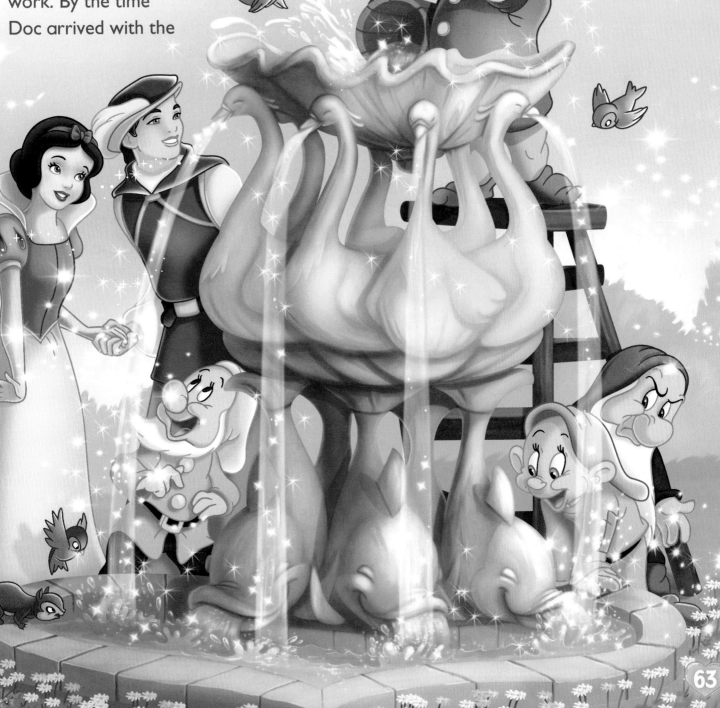

Garden Dance

Look closely at this picture of Snow White and the Prince and answer the questions.

How many butterflies can you count?

Can you find three heart shapes hidden in the picture?

Where is the little deer hiding?

How many birds can you count?

Answers: There are eight butterflies. The deer is hiding by the well. There is one heart in the clouds, one on the wishing well and one blue heart-shaped flower. There are five birds.

Pretty Picture

Bring this gorgeous Snow White picture to life with some beautiful colours!

Sunny Scene

Can you spot the six differences in the
second picture of Snow White and her friends?
Colour an apple each time you find one.

1

2

Answers: Snow White's hairband is green, a deer has appeared, a chipmunk has appeared,
Grumpy's hat is blue, a pink bird has disappeared and a blue bird has disappeared.

Magical Princess Style

What's your princess style? Tick the item in each group that you like best, then look below to find out which princess is your style icon!

Sparkling Shoes

Dreamy Dresses

Mostly Purple

You adore Jasmine's pretty style. Lots of gorgeous gem colours, like greens and purples, really make you sparkle and cute flat slippers would look so sweet on your petite feet!

Mostly Blue

Cinderella's glittering wardrobe is full of beautiful powder blue accessories and dresses. It would be your dream come true to dress up in her gorgeous gowns and glass slippers!

Beautiful Bags

Terrific Tiaras

If you chose one of each colour or two pairs, your style is a dazzling princess mix!

Mostly Pink

Like Aurora, you're girly and dreamy and pink is your favourite colour. If you were a princess, you'd love to wear a stunning gold tiara and a delicate pink gown, too!

Mostly Yellow

Your style is most like Belle's. You love bright, beautiful yellow to match your sunny personality and pretty matching accessories with flowers and bows are the best!